Celebrating Sunday
for Catholic
Families
2017–2018

Kerstin Keber Smith

LTP

LITURGY
TRAINING
PUBLICATIONS

Nihil Obstat
Very Reverend Daniel A. Smilanic, JCD
Vicar for Canonical Services
Archdiocese of Chicago
July 29, 2016

Imprimatur
Very Reverend Ronald A. Hicks
Vicar General
Archdiocese of Chicago
July 29, 2016

CELEBRATING SUNDAY FOR CATHOLIC FAMILIES 2017–2018 © 2017
Archdiocese of Chicago: Liturgy Training Publications, 3949 South Racine
Avenue, Chicago, IL 60609; 1-800-933-1800; fax 1-800-933-7094; e-mail:
orders@ltp.org; website: www.LTP.org. All rights reserved.

This book was edited by Mary Fox. Christopher Magnus was the production editor, Anna Manhart was the designer, and Kari Nicholls was the
production artist.

Cover illustration by Eleanor Davis © LTP.

Printed in the United States of America.

ISBN 978-1-61671-328-7

CSCF18

"You shall love the LORD your God with all your heart, and with all your soul, and with all your might. Keep these words that I am commanding to you today in your heart. Recite them to your children and talk about them when you are at home and when you are away, when you lie down and when you rise."

(Deuteronomy 6:5–7)

Contents

How to Use

Celebrating Sunday for Catholic Families

This small weekly guide draws on the Gospel for each Sunday and Holyday for the coming year. It is intended to help parents engage their children with the Mass and deepen their appreciation of the richness of their faith life. So often, going to Mass becomes a weekly event that begins and ends at the church door. The brief reflection for the parent on an excerpt from the Gospel is intended to spark his or her thinking about the Scripture that will lead to conversation with the family on the way to and from Mass. Suggestions for questions and conversation starters are provided, as well as some practice or practical way to carry this reflection into the life of the family.

We hope that many of the reflections and suggestions will enrich your family's life of faith. Some weeks, you may have other needs, concerns, or ideas that fit your life. If so, engage your children with those. A note about very young children: They are very able to enter into the liturgy through their senses. Singing the hymns, calling their attention to the changing colors of the liturgical seasons, and sitting where they can observe the gestures of the Mass are all ways to form them in the faith. Always remember, as the Rite of Baptism proclaims, you, as parents, are your children's first and most important teachers.

September 10, 2017

Twenty-Third Sunday in Ordinary Time

Hearing the Word

Matthew 18:15–17

In the name of the Father, and of the Son, and of the Holy Spirit.

Jesus said to his disciples: "If your brother sins against you, go and tell him his fault between you and him alone. If he listens to you, you have won over your brother. If he does not listen, take one or two others along with you, so that 'every fact may be established on the testimony of two or three witnesses.' If he refuses to listen to them, tell the church. If he refuses to listen even to the church, then treat him as you would a Gentile or a tax collector."

Reflecting on the Word

It is hard when we feel that someone is not listening to us, especially when we have been hurt. It is important to remember we are not alone when something like this happens. We can go to people who will help and support us. When people hurt others, they are usually hurt themselves. When we can bring them into the love and support of the community, often they are able to see things differently.

•••••• ON THE WAY TO MASS:

Can you recall a time when you did not feel listened to? How did it make you feel?

ON THE WAY HOME FROM MASS: ••••••

Why is it helpful to have a community like the Church when people won't listen to what is right?

Living the Word

Gather the family and discuss how you can each try harder to listen this week. Suggest that they resolve to listen, even if someone is telling a story they have heard before. They can try to see why the story is important. They can listen more to family members and seek to understand the other person when they disagree. Listening can even include going outside and being present in nature. Provide pencils and paper for everyone to make a list of or draw ways they can listen better.

September 17, 2017

Twenty-Fourth Sunday in Ordinary Time

Hearing the Word

Matthew 18:21–22

In the name of the Father, and of the Son, and of the Holy Spirit.

Peter approached Jesus and asked him, "Lord, if my brother sins against me, how often must I forgive? As many as seven times?" Jesus answered, "I say to you, not seven times but seventy-seven times."

Reflecting on the Word

Forgiveness can be hard, whether we are giving it or receiving it. We do not like to feel that we have done something wrong, but all of us sometimes need forgiveness. It can help to remember our failings when others are unkind. In these times, we need to rely on the deepest parts of our hearts that are connected to God. In that place we will always be able to find the strength and patience to forgive, even if it is seventy-seven times.

······ON THE WAY TO MASS:

Can you remember a time when you needed to be forgiven? How did the person you hurt respond?

ON THE WAY HOME FROM MASS: ······

Is there someone you need to forgive, but it seems too hard to do so? What would help make it easier?

Living the Word

Ask family members to try on the skin of a forgiving person today. Tell them to see if, for one day, they can forgive big and little things that happen. At the end of the day, ask them: How do you feel? Will it be easier to go to sleep at night? Did you find your day went smoother since you weren't focusing on the bad things but the goodness of God's forgiveness? What things were harder than others to forgive? Is this a practice you could keep up?

September 24, 2017

Twenty-Fifth Sunday in Ordinary Time

Hearing the Word

Matthew 20:8–15

"When it was evening, the owner of the vineyard said to his foreman, 'Summon the laborers and give them their pay, beginning with the last and ending with the first.' When those who had started about five o'clock came, each received the usual daily wage. So when the first came, they thought that they would receive more, but each of them also got the usual wage. And on receiving it they grumbled against the landowner, saying, 'These last ones worked only one hour, and you have made them equal to us, who bore the day's burden and the heat.' He said to one of them in reply, 'My friend, I am not cheating you. Did you not agree with me for the usual daily wage? Take what is yours and go. Are you envious because I am generous?'"

Reflecting on the Word

God's love is so wonderful and powerful that we would not want anyone to miss out on it, no matter when they discover it. If God is like the landowner, then we want people to be able to come to him whenever they are ready. We are grateful that God's love has no limit, and it is available to all. With God, just because my brother or sister receives "payment," it does not lessen the amount I get and so in God's abundance we all get what we need.

•••••• ON THE WAY TO MASS:

What does it mean to be fair? How is this different from being generous?

ON THE WAY HOME FROM MASS: ••••••

When and where have you experienced God's loving abundance?

Living the Word

Talk to your family about inviting someone to the "vineyard" of God's love. Everyone could brainstorm, considering if a friend, neighbor, or family member might feel left out. Make plans this week to invite that person(s) to lunch, the park, or your house. What can you do to show the unlimited abundance of God's love? Tell them to remember that God's love is a gift that is given to us, no matter what we have done or where we have been.

Twenty-Sixth Sunday in Ordinary Time

Hearing the Word

Matthew 21:28–31

In the name of the Father, and of the Son, and of the Holy Spirit.

"What is your opinion? A man had two sons. He came to the first and said, 'Son, go out and work in the vineyard today.' He said in reply, 'I will not,' but afterwards changed his mind and went. The man came to the other son and gave the same order. He said in reply, 'Yes, sir,' but did not go. Which of the two did his father's will?" They answered, "The first." Jesus said to them, "Amen, I say to you, tax collectors and prostitutes are entering the kingdom of God before you."

Reflecting on the Word

What we say and what we do are sometimes different. Jesus points out that both are important but what we do and the way we act in the world will have the larger impact. This story also shows us that it is never too late to act. If our initial response to something is not in line with God's will, we can change our response. We can always revisit our decisions and ways of being and correct them if necessary. No matter what we have done, we can always return to God.

......ON THE WAY TO MASS:

Have you ever changed your mind? Why? How did you come to a different conclusion?

ON THE WAY HOME FROM MASS: ......

Have you ever been surprised that someone was doing God's work?

Living the Word

Light a candle in your prayer space and talk to your family about how aligning our words with our hearts is hard but necessary work. Often words come out of our mouths before we have had a chance to think about them, and sometimes our actions are automatic. Decide as a family to try to say what Jesus would and then do those things. At the end of the day, gather again and hear each family member report back on the experiment. Ask the children if they listened to the words of others differently.

Twenty-Seventh Sunday in Ordinary Time

Hearing the Word

Matthew 21:33–35, 37–41

In the name of the Father, and of the Son, and of the Holy Spirit.

"There was a landowner who planted a vineyard, put a hedge around it, dug a wine press in it, and built a tower. Then he leased it to tenants and went on a journey. When vintage time drew near, he sent his servants to the tenants to obtain his produce. But the tenants seized the servants and one they beat, another they killed, and a third they stoned. Finally, he sent his son to them, thinking, 'They will respect my son.' They seized him, threw him out of the vineyard, and killed him. What will the owner of the vineyard do to those tenants when he comes?" They answered him, "He will put those wretched men to a wretched death and lease his vineyard to other tenants who will give him the produce at the proper times."

Reflecting on the Word

Now this story is rough! We don't want to hear how violent we human beings can be. While we may not have beat people, we have hurt others through a look, a word, even a thought. The harshness of our words and actions have consequences. All the world and its inhabitants are a gift and we must be kind and compassionate to those in our care. Otherwise, Jesus tells us, the vineyard will go to those who will honor and respect it. We must care for each gift from God.

······ ON THE WAY TO MASS:

In what way could you be gentler with the earth, people, plants, and animals?

ON THE WAY HOME FROM MASS: ······

Where has violence crept into your life and you haven't even noticed it? In your speech, video games, TV shows, etc?

Living the Word

Expressing kindness and care in our words and actions takes practice and intention. Choose something to do as a family (a special meal, a game, an outing, a car ride) and for the duration of that event, each person will only use a whisper voice. Ask the family members to notice how a gentle voice tends to bring about gentle actions. Notice how words sound differently when whispered.

Twenty-Eighth Sunday in Ordinary Time

Hearing the Word

Matthew 22:8–10

In the name of the Father, and of the Son, and of the Holy Spirit.

"Then he said to his servants, 'The feast is ready, but those who were invited were not worthy to come. Go out, therefore, into the main roads and invite to the feast whomever you find.' The servants went out into the streets and gathered all they found, bad and good alike, and the hall was filled with guests."

Reflecting on the Word

There is room for all at God's table, but will all accept the invitation? In this story, we see that acceptance requires more than just showing up. We have to come prepared and worthy, and those who have more notice, have more responsibility. Even though we need to be ready at any moment to come as we are, we should prepare for what we know is coming. While these seem like opposites, they both require an ability to be alert and ready for God's feast. Consider *this* your notice!

••••••ON THE WAY TO MASS:

Have you ever been underprepared for an event? How did it feel? What was the outcome?

ON THE WAY HOME FROM MASS: ••••••

How can we be more inviting in our sharing with others?

Living the Word

Ask the family member who sets the table to set an extra space. Encourage everyone to takes turns imagining who might be invited to that chair. (It needs to be someone who has never sat at the table before.) Imagine how the person might feel sitting with you. Help everyone think of how you would make the person feel welcome. Then, invite someone for a special meal. Even if the person cannot come, notice the feelings that come with being invited.

Twenty-Ninth Sunday in Ordinary Time

Hearing the Word
Matthew 22:15, 17–21

In the name of the Father, and of the Son, and of the Holy Spirit.

The Pharisees . . . plotted how they might entrap Jesus
in speech, . . . saying, "Tell us, then, what is your opinion:
Is it lawful to pay the census tax to Caesar or not?" Knowing
their malice, Jesus said, "Why are you testing me, you
hypocrites? Show me the coin that pays the census tax."
Then they handed him the Roman coin. He said to them,
"Whose image is this and whose inscription?" They
replied, "Caesar's." At that he said to them, "Then repay
to Caesar what belongs to Caesar and to God what belongs
to God."

Reflecting on the Word

We see the sneaky Pharisees trying to catch Jesus in a trap. They do not succeed, however. There is no way to get around the truth; it will always prevail. Over and over, Jesus reminds us to think outside the box and not compromise our values or our ability to be present and a force for good in society. Instead of going against the law of the land, he finds a way within it to assert the primacy of God.

• • • • • • ON THE WAY TO MASS:

Have you ever felt caught in a trap? Where did you turn for help?

ON THE WAY HOME FROM MASS: • • • • • •

Is there a way to reflect the sacred in the way you live? How?

Living the Word

After lighting a candle, say a prayer with the family. Tell your children that there have always been clashes between civic law and what "belongs to God." In today's Gospel, it is interesting that Jesus does not make a strict separation between the two. He says that we are to give what is due in each realm. The best thing is to live out the sacred *in* the secular. Encourage your family to discuss how doing home-work and chores can reflect the love of God.

October 29, 2017

Thirtieth Sunday in Ordinary Time

Hearing the Word

Matthew 22:36–40

In the name of the Father, and of the Son, and of the Holy Spirit.

"Teacher, which commandment in the law is the greatest?" He said to him, "You shall love the Lord, your God, with all your heart, with all your soul, and with all your mind. This is the greatest and the first commandment. The second is like it: You shall love your neighbor as yourself. The whole law and the prophets depend on these two commandments."

Reflecting on the Word

There are no laws, rules, or even talents and merits that can surpass love. Love for God, others, and self should be all-consuming. It should pervade our hearts, minds, and souls so much there is no space for anything else. The way Jesus spoke of the commandments gives us a clue as to how to live them. Instead of giving a list of what not to do, he tells us to focus on what and who we should be. When this becomes our focus, there is room for nothing else in our life but love!

•••••• ON THE WAY TO MASS:

What would it look like to love with your whole heart, mind, and soul?

ON THE WAY HOME FROM MASS: ••••••

How do you show love to yourself?

Living the Word

Bring the family into the prayer space and discuss how doing God's will starts with loving ourselves. Encourage family members to pay attention to the way they talk to themselves this week. Ask them to think about whether they love themselves the way God loves them, or if they criticize themselves. Next, everybody should write down something kind to say to a person with whom they have had a hard time getting along. Can the family think of a time to say these brave and kind words?

Solemnity of All Saints

Hearing the Word

Matthew 5:1–12a

In the name of the Father, and of the Son, and of the Holy Spirit.

When Jesus saw the crowds, he went up the mountain, and after he had sat down, his disciples came to him. He began to teach them, saying: / "Blessed are the poor in spirit, / for theirs is the Kingdom of heaven. / Blessed are they who mourn, / for they will be comforted. / Blessed are the meek, / for they will inherit the land. / Blessed are they who hunger and thirst for righteousness, / for they will be satisfied. / Blessed are the merciful, / for they will be shown mercy. / Blessed are the clean of heart, / for they will see God. / Blessed are the peacemakers, / for they will be called children of God. / Blessed are they who are persecuted for the sake of righteousness, / for theirs is the Kingdom of heaven. / Blessed are you when they insult you and persecute you / and utter every kind of evil against you falsely because of me. / Rejoice and be glad, / for your reward will be great in heaven."

Reflecting on the Word

It might be hard to find the Beatitudes as a reason to rejoice. Some may even think that Jesus can keep his reward if recipients first need to mourn or be persecuted. Jesus may be asking us to look again at the hard things in life. Can there be joy in mourning, hunger, and persecution? Do we have the ability to return to God's love repeatedly and live out of that love, while still recognizing the pain and suffering that we endure as part of being on earth?

•••••• ON THE WAY TO MASS:

Has anyone shown mercy to you?

ON THE WAY HOME FROM MASS: ••••••

What does it mean to be blessed? To feel blessed?

Living the Word

Decide as a family how you will adopt an attitude of gratitude this week. During the nightly prayer, encourage the children to thank God for a specific thing, event, or person instead of asking for something. At breakfast, invite the children to share one "thankful" thing and see how starting their day this way changes their outlook. If this is a particularly hard week for the family, reflect on how certain blessings help you get through hard times.

November 5, 2017

THIRTY-FIRST SUNDAY IN ORDINARY TIME

Hearing the Word

Matthew 23:1, 8–12

In the name of the Father, and of the Son, and of the Holy Spirit.

Jesus spoke to the crowds and to his disciples, saying, "As for you, do not be called 'Rabbi.' You have but one teacher, and you are all brothers. Call no one on earth your father; you have but one Father in heaven. Do not be called 'Master'; you have but one master, the Christ. The greatest among you must be your servant. Whoever exalts himself will be humbled; but whoever humbles himself will be exalted."

Reflecting on the Word

The impermanence of our earthly lives is reinforced in these simple but intense statements. Life began before we were born and will continue after, so earthly parents claiming that place permanently in our souls does not hold up when we consider the enormity of God and our infinite existence. There is no true teacher, master, or parent but God. Still, we can honor the reflection of God's love and wisdom in those around us while still realizing they pale in comparison.

······ ON THE WAY TO MASS:

Where do you see the parents, teachers, and bosses in your life reflecting God's love and wisdom?

ON THE WAY HOME FROM MASS: ······

What does it mean to be humble? What does it mean to be exalted? Are they always opposites?

Living the Word

Discuss how Jesus lived the virtue of humility. Ask the children if they think humility is important. What does it feel like to be the greatest at something? What does that mean in heaven? Encourage everyone to try the following experiment this week: the next time you stand at the front of a line, give up your place to someone else and go to the back. Notice how it feels to choose to be at the back. Is waiting different when you know you gave up your spot?

November 12, 2017

Thirty-Second Sunday in Ordinary Time

Hearing the Word

Matthew 25:1–13

In the name of the Father, and of the Son, and of the Holy Spirit.

Jesus told his disciples this parable: "The kingdom of heaven will be like ten virgins who took their lamps and went out to meet the bridegroom. Five of them were foolish and five were wise. The foolish ones, when taking their lamps, brought no oil with them, but the wise brought flasks of oil with their lamps. Since the bridegroom was long delayed, they all became drowsy and fell asleep. At midnight, there was a cry, 'Behold, the bridegroom! Come out to meet him!' Then all those virgins got up and trimmed their lamps. The foolish ones said to the wise, 'Give us some of your oil, for our lamps are going out.' But the wise ones replied, 'No, for there may not be enough for us and you. Go instead to the merchants and buy some for yourselves.' While they went off to buy it, the bridegroom came and those who were ready went into the wedding feast with him. Then the door was locked. Afterwards the other virgins came and said, 'Lord, Lord, open the door for us!' But he said in reply, 'Amen, I say to you, I do not know you.' Therefore, stay awake, for you know neither the day nor the hour."

Reflecting on the Word

As we get closer to Advent the readings seek to awaken us. Jesus makes it clear that the joys of heaven are not a given, but nor do we have to earn them. Rather, we have to be ready and present. The gift is already given but we need to be prepared to receive it. Attentiveness brings us to live more fully in each moment instead of focusing on the past or the future. Nothing is a given and not even the past is static as our experiences are constantly changed by our present interactions.

• • • • • • ON THE WAY TO MASS:

Why is it good to be prepared?

ON THE WAY HOME FROM MASS: • • • • • •

What are some things that need more of your attention?

Living the Word

Light a candle in your prayer space and discuss the preparation needed for a trip out of town. Encourage the children to think of all the things that are done when leaving home even for a weekend. Then, ask each family member to think about how they would prepare to see God. Ask: What preparation is needed to go to heaven? How are you preparing for that now? Is there anything else you should do? How will Advent help you prepare to see God some day?

November 19, 2017

Thirty-Third Sunday in Ordinary Time

Hearing the Word

Matthew 25:14–15, 19–21

In the name of the Father, and of the Son, and of the Holy Spirit.

Jesus told his disciples this parable: "A man going on a journey called in his servants and entrusted his possessions to them. To one he gave five talents; to another, two; to a third, one—to each according to his ability. Then he went away.

"After a long time the master of those servants came back and settled accounts with them. The one who had received five talents came forward bringing the additional five. He said, 'Master, you gave me five talents. See, I have made five more.' His master said to him, 'Well done, my good and faithful servant. Since you were faithful in small matters, I will give you great responsibilities. Come, share your master's joy.'"

Reflecting on the Word

Our gifts are given to us to be used. However, it can be scary that the offer of our gifts will be rejected. What we see in this story is that God will make our gifts more bountiful when we use them. Our gifts will not grow unless they are used. Sometimes, it takes a while to discover our strengths and talents, but when we do, they will bring abundance to us and others as well.

･･････ON THE WAY TO MASS:

Name one of your gifts and how you can use it today.

ON THE WAY HOME FROM MASS: ･･････

Are you ever afraid of using your gifts?

Living the Word

At the family prayer space, discuss how using our gifts can be scary. One of the scariest things about using our gifts is that we may actually succeed at what we have set out to do. As you imagine your gifts growing, write or draw things that could stand in the way of using your gifts to their fullest. Invite the children to share how they feel about the obstacles. Take a moment to work through those emotions together and then encourage the children to dispose of the obstacles by giving them over to God.

November 26, 2017

Solemnity of Our Lord Jesus Christ, King of the Universe

Hearing the Word

Matthew 25:31–34

In the name of the Father, and of the Son, and of the Holy Spirit.

Jesus said to his disciples: "When the Son of Man comes in his glory, and all the angels with him, he will sit upon his glorious throne, and all the nations will be assembled before him. And he will separate them one from another, as a shepherd separates the sheep from the goats. He will place the sheep on his right and the goats on his left. Then the king will say to those on his right, 'Come, you who are blessed by my Father. Inherit the kingdom prepared for you from the foundation of the world.'"

Reflecting on the Word

Recognizing Christ as King reminds us of our baptismal call and our anointing at Baptism. Made in the image of God, we gave a promise through our Baptism to reflect the divine in all we do. When we pay attention to this call, people will be attracted to the spark of divinity that shines through us. Proudly wear the crown you were born with and the difference in you will be as clear as separating sheep from goats.

......ON THE WAY TO MASS:

How do you reflect God in everyday situations?

ON THE WAY HOME FROM MASS: ......

In what way does God's love rule in your heart?

Living the Word

Have a royal dinner tonight and invite everyone to dress up in formal attire. If the family would like to do so, they can even make crowns to wear and decorate. Recognizing that God always reigns supreme, talk about how we can be instruments of God's love on earth. As kings and queens we have a responsibility to take care of all that God has given us as well as to live justly and honestly. To conclude the meal, have each family make a "royal decree" of how God's love will be lived through them.

December 3, 2017

First Sunday of Advent

Hearing the Word

Mark 13:33–37

In the name of the Father, and of the Son, and of the Holy Spirit.

Jesus said to his disciples: "Be watchful! Be alert! You do not know when the time will come. It is like a man traveling abroad. He leaves home and places his servants in charge, each with his own work, and orders the gatekeeper to be on the watch. Watch, therefore; you do not know when the Lord of the house is coming, whether in the evening, or at midnight, or at cockcrow, or in the morning. May he not come suddenly and find you sleeping. What I say to you, I say to all: 'Watch!'"

Reflecting on the Word

The words of an Advent song remind us to "Stay awake! Be ready!" Awake in this case means to be watchful just as the gatekeepers in today's Gospel needed to be. Such attentiveness requires a never-ending amount of patience. However, patience does not come easily in a society where fast food and instant communication are expected. Advent calls us to cultivate patience as we seek the ways of the Lord in our daily lives. Are you able to be alert to God stirring among you?

•••••• ON THE WAY TO MASS:

What are you waiting for?

ON THE WAY HOME FROM MASS: ••••••

How can you use this time of Advent to watchfully prepare for Christ's coming?

Living the Word

Light a candle and decide as a family how you can visibly wait for Christmas. You could wait to put out the red and green of Christmas and instead decorate with deep purples. You can make an Advent wreath as a family and each night light a candle. You may wait to put up the tree, or progressively decorate it. Start with the lights, then the next week add the star, then some tinsel, and in the last week of Advent, add some ornaments daily until you are ready for Christmas.

Solemnity of the Immaculate Conception of the Blessed Virgin Mary

Luke 1:26–38

In the name of the Father, and of the Son, and of the Holy Spirit.

The angel Gabriel was sent from God to a town of Galilee called Nazareth, to a virgin betrothed to a man named Joseph, of the house of David, and the virgin's name was Mary. And coming to her, he said, "Hail, full of grace! The Lord is with you." But she was greatly troubled at what was said and pondered what sort of greeting this might be. Then the angel said to her, "Do not be afraid, Mary, for you have found favor with God. Behold, you will conceive in your womb and bear a son, and you shall name him Jesus. He will be great and will be called Son of the Most High, and the Lord God will give him the throne of David his father, and he will rule over the house of Jacob forever, and of his Kingdom there will be no end." But Mary said to the angel, "How can this be, since I have no relations with a man?" And the angel said to her in reply, "The Holy Spirit will come upon you, and the power of the Most High will overshadow you. Therefore the child to be born will be called holy, the Son of God. And behold, Elizabeth, your relative, has also conceived a son in her old age, and this is the sixth month for her who was called barren; for nothing will be impossible for God." Mary said, "Behold, I am the handmaid of the Lord. May it be done to me according to your word." Then the angel departed from her.

Reflecting on the Word

As we celebrate Mary's coming into being, we are reminded why. Mary carried the Body and Blood of Jesus in her womb and birthed him into the world. Her commitment to an emptying of herself, her plans, and her dreams, allowed her to be full of nothing but the Holy Spirit. Her power and grace made possible Christ's coming in such a completely unassuming and effective way. Through Mary, God was able to be truly and fully with us in our humanity.

•••••• ON THE WAY TO MASS:

What could you empty yourself of to make more space for the Holy Spirit?

ON THE WAY HOME FROM MASS: ••••••

Have you ever said "Yes!" to God? How did it go?

Living the Word

Light a candle after gathering the family in the prayer space. Encourage everyone to think about how we often say "no" when asked to do something. Invite them this week to say "yes" to something that they would not normally. You might want to discuss how it can be scary to say "yes" sometimes. For some things, the children might want to discuss with family members their hesitation to say "yes." Remind them that Mary's "yes" changed the course of her life.

December 10, 2017

SECOND SUNDAY OF ADVENT

Hearing the Word
Mark 1:1–5, 7–8

In the name of the Father, and of the Son, and of the Holy Spirit.

The beginning of the gospel of Jesus Christ the Son of God.

As it is written in Isaiah the prophet: / *Behold, I am sending my messenger ahead of you; / he will prepare your way. / A voice of one crying out in the desert: / "Prepare the way of the Lord, / make straight his paths."* / John the Baptist appeared in the desert proclaiming a baptism of repentance for the forgiveness of sins. People of the whole Judean countryside and all the inhabitants of Jerusalem were going out to him and were being baptized by him in the Jordan River as they acknowledged their sins. . . . And this is what he proclaimed: "One mightier than I is coming after me. I am not worthy to stoop and loosen the thongs of his sandals. I have baptized you with water; he will baptize you with the Holy Spirit."

Reflecting on the Word

John the Baptist is a wonderful reminder of our ability and necessity to be present in the Christ story as it unfolds today. The path is still not completely clear. We are being called to proclaim the forgiveness of sins today more than ever. This ongoing preparation takes place in the gentle turning of hearts and minds of all we meet toward the love and acceptance of God. In this time of darkness, we are called to be light for one another.

•••••• ON THE WAY TO MASS:

Do you feel prepared to meet Christ if he showed up today?

ON THE WAY HOME FROM MASS: ••••••

How can we be a light in a world that often looks so dark?

Living the Word

Bring the light into your home tonight. As a family, make or decorate a special candle or candle holder that you can light at the dinner table to bring warmth and cheer in this time of darkness. Let it stand as a reminder of the constant need for preparation in our hearts and minds. You could use bits of tissue paper and a mixture of glue and water or mod podge to cover the outside of a glass jar, creating a stained-glass effect when a votive candle is placed inside.

Third Sunday of Advent

Hearing the Word

John 1:6–8, 23–28

In the name of the Father, and of the Son, and of the Holy Spirit.

A man named John was sent from God. He came for testimony, to testify to the light, so that all might believe through him. He was not the light, but came to testify to the light. . . .

[John] said: "I am *the voice of one crying in the desert, 'Make straight the way of the Lord,'* as Isaiah the prophet said." Some Pharisees were also sent. They asked him, "Why, then, do you baptize if you are not the Christ or Elijah or the Prophet?" John answered them, "I baptize with water; but there is one among you whom you do not recognize, the one who is coming after me, whose sandal strap I am not worthy to untie." This happened in Bethany across the Jordan where John was baptizing.

Reflecting on the Word

John clearly shows us that we are not meant to be the light ourselves, but rather reflect the light of Christ. Even as great as John was at the time and for all the followers he had, he knew that it was not he but the one he spoke of that attracted people. The realization of our unworthiness ensures our message and actions are in service to God. Coming back to this again and again will enable us to help others along the way. If you speak Christ's words, people will listen.

• • • • • • ON THE WAY TO MASS:

Share a time when you clearly felt your actions and words were a reflection of Christ.

ON THE WAY HOME FROM MASS: • • • • • •

What were some of the ways the church service today reflected Christ's light in deed and symbol?

Living the Word

To reflect on the ways family members can be light to each other and reflect the love of God in all they say and do, the family can create a collage of light. In these final days leading up to Christmas, dedicate a space in your home where family members can hang or place paper candles with the deeds or words of others that bring warmth and light. There is no limit to the number that the family can put up in a day. Ask your children how the candles make them feel.

December 24, 2017

Fourth Sunday of Advent

Hearing the Word
Luke 1:26–28

In the name of the Father, and of the Son, and of the Holy Spirit.

The angel Gabriel was sent from God to a town of Galilee
called Nazareth, to a virgin betrothed to a man named
Joseph, of the house of David, and the virgin's name
was Mary. And coming to her, he said, "Hail, full of grace!
The Lord is with you."

Reflecting on the Word

As we prepare to celebrate Christmas tomorrow we recognize that the world is imperfect just as it was when Gabriel
came to Mary, and Jesus came to the world. Ready or not,
Christ is on his way and our level of preparation will determine just how *much* we are able to receive. Jesus did not
wait for the darkness to disappear to arrive; he came right
in the middle of it and filled it with light! May the Lord also
be with you as you make your final preparations to welcome
the Christ Child.

•••••• ON THE WAY TO MASS:

If you were Gabriel, how would you have greeted Mary?

ON THE WAY HOME FROM MASS: ••••••

What kind of message do you think your Guardian Angel has
for you?

Living the Word

Invite each family member to send an angel message
to another family member today. Draw names and give
everyone time to construct a special angel message.
These messages could be placed under the Christmas tree
or in a stocking. The messages may be communicated by
word or picture and should have three parts: (1) a greeting
(such as, Hail *name* full of joy, humor, love, *or another
description*); (2) a blessing (Blessed are you for your_____.);
and (3) a special Christmas message. These messages can
be hung in a prominent place for the Christmas season.

December 25, 2017

Solemnity of the Nativity of the Lord

Hearing the Word
John 1:1–5, 14

In the name of the Father, and of the Son, and of the Holy Spirit.

In the beginning was the Word, / and the Word was with God, / and the Word was God. / He was in the beginning with God. / All things came to be through him, / and without him nothing came to be. / What came to be through him was life, / and this life was the light of the human race; / the light shines in the darkness, / and the darkness has not overcome it.

And the Word became flesh / and made his dwelling among us, / and we saw his glory, / the glory as of the Father's only Son, / full of grace and truth. /

Reflecting on the Word

That God would send God's only son to be a light here among us is impossible to fully wrap our minds around. Filling the darkness with light makes the presence of darkness obsolete. This means we do not need to control our environment, but simply shine within it; for where the light is, there is no room for the darkness to grow and it will continue to shrink to the corners of our existence until it cannot find refuge. One single light can fill a room and one single life can heal a world.

• • • • • • ON THE WAY TO MASS:

Are you afraid of the dark? Why or why not?

ON THE WAY HOME FROM MASS: • • • • • •

What is your favorite Christmas tradition? Is there another one you would like to add?

Living the Word

Today we celebrate the Word Made Flesh. Each family member should choose a word to share that is a reminder of Christ's light. Each time the word is said, the person can fold hands in prayer for a mini-blessing. See if you can catch another family member saying the word. Make a game of how many times you can use the word in an hour, a sentence, during dinner, etc. Notice how powerful these words are to simply say and imagine them if they were actually living and breathing people. What would they look like? How would you treat them?

December 31, 2017

Feast of the Holy Family of Jesus, Mary, and Joseph

Hearing the Word

Luke 2:22, 39–40

In the name of the Father, and of the Son, and of the Holy Spirit.

When the days were completed for their purification according to the law of Moses, they took him up to Jerusalem to present him to the Lord.

When they had fulfilled all the prescriptions of the law of the Lord, they returned to Galilee, to their own town of Nazareth. The child grew and became strong, filled with wisdom; and the favor of God was upon him.

Reflecting on the Word

We can look to Mary and Joseph as parents who took the time to observe the practices that are part of their faith. Passing on the faith was important to the holy family. Often, parents feel too busy to take their children to Mass and teach them their prayers. But Mary and Joseph took a break from their routine to observe the practices of Judaism.

• • • • • • ON THE WAY TO MASS:

Why is your religion important to you?

ON THE WAY HOME FROM MASS: • • • • • •

Why do we go to Mass?

Living the Word

Discuss with the children the value your family placed on the faith while you were growing up. Tell them about some of the ways your household practiced the faith. Determine a new way that your family will do so. Perhaps you will begin to pray before or after meals or say an evening prayer together.

January 7, 2018

Solemnity of the Epiphany of the Lord

Hearing the Word

Matthew 2:7–12

In the name of the Father, and of the Son, and of the Holy Spirit.

Then Herod called the magi secretly and ascertained from them the time of the star's appearance. He sent them to Bethlehem and said, "Go and search diligently for the child. When you have found him, bring me word, that I too may go and do him homage." After their audience with the king they set out. And behold, the star that they had seen at its rising preceded them, until it came and stopped over the place where the child was. They were overjoyed at seeing the star, and on entering the house they saw the child with Mary his mother. They prostrated themselves and did him homage. Then they opened their treasures and offered him gifts of gold, frankincense, and myrrh. And having been warned in a dream not to return to Herod, they departed for their country by another way.

Reflecting on the Word

The presence of the Magi illustrates that Jesus came to heal the world, not just a select group of people. These travelers from afar show just how powerful the message of hope and forgiveness is. God reaches out with love to all people without regard to their country of origin.

• • • • • • ON THE WAY TO MASS:

Why did people travel from far away to see the baby Jesus?

ON THE WAY HOME FROM MASS: • • • • • • •

What does the word *epiphany* mean to you?

Living the Word

The Magi navigated by the light of a star, and so invite your family to be in the dark tonight. Notice what it is like to be without artificial light. After your eyes have adjusted, choose one person to be the "star" and light up the room with a single light. See how quickly you can get to them. The person to make it there first will be the next "star" and so on. Spend some time reflecting on how much longer the journey of the Magi was and how exciting it must have been to finally reach Jesus.

SECOND SUNDAY IN ORDINARY TIME

Hearing the Word

John 1:35–42

In the name of the Father, and of the Son, and of the Holy Spirit.

John was standing with two of his disciples, and as he watched Jesus walk by, he said, "Behold, the Lamb of God." The two disciples heard what he said and followed Jesus. Jesus turned and saw them following him and said to them, "What are you looking for?" They said to him, "Rabbi"—which translated means Teacher—, "where are you staying?" He said to them, "Come, and you will see." So they went and saw where he was staying, and they stayed with him that day. It was about four in the afternoon. Andrew, the brother of Simon Peter, was one of the two who heard John and followed Jesus. He first found his own brother Simon and told him, "We have found the Messiah"—which is translated Christ—. Then he brought him to Jesus. Jesus looked at him and said, "You are Simon the son of John; you will be called Cephas"—which is translated Peter.

Reflecting on the Word

As the Church returns to Ordinary Time, we are met with the excitement of the disciples as they recognize and follow Jesus. Ordinary Time in the liturgical year is anything but typical or "ordinary." While we return to the color green and move away from the excitement of the manger, we are met with stories about the ministry of Jesus. As we hear of Jesus' teaching and healing, we learn what it means to be daughters and sons of God. It is in the "ordinary time" that our lives our truly lived out and our missions completed.

•••••• ON THE WAY TO MASS:

What is something extraordinary about the ordinary in your life?

ON THE WAY HOME FROM MASS: ••••••

What did you notice about the way the church looked as compared to the Advent and Christmas seasons?

Living the Word

With your family, look back through this passage at the many promises God makes us through the names that Jesus is called. Words and phrases like *Rabbi* and *Messiah,* and the *Lamb of God* stand out. Using the Bible, see if you can find more images or phrases to describe God. (Hint: Jesus uses many in his parables.) Invite each family member to depict an image through action, a poem, or a drawing. Come together to share your reflections. Encourage family members to explain why they chose a word or phrase.

January 21, 2018

THIRD SUNDAY IN ORDINARY TIME

Hearing the Word

Mark 1:14–20

In the name of the Father, and of the Son, and of the Holy Spirit.

After John had been arrested, Jesus came to Galilee proclaiming the gospel of God: "This is the time of fulfillment. The kingdom of God is at hand. Repent, and believe in the gospel."

As he passed by the Sea of Galilee, he saw Simon and his brother Andrew casting their nets into the sea; they were fishermen. Jesus said to them, "Come after me, and I will make you fishers of men." Then they abandoned their nets and followed him. He walked along a little farther and saw James, the son of Zebedee, and his brother John. They too were in a boat mending their nets. Then he called them. So they left their father Zebedee in the boat along with the hired men and followed him.

Reflecting on the Word

If you want to catch fish, you need the right equipment, you must go where the fish are and have plenty of patience! We cannot expect people to knock down our door to hear Christ's message, we have to go and meet them equipped with our knowledge of the Bible and our faith. Many will not be interested or ready to hear the Good News, and that is where we practice patience. If Jesus only came for those who were ready to enter heaven's gates, then what would be the point? We must gently and lovingly keep guiding all toward his message of peace and love.

······ ON THE WAY TO MASS:

What do you need to be able to catch fish?

ON THE WAY HOME FROM MASS: ······

How has God called you to be a fisher of people? What equipment do you still need?

Living the Word

Jesus had so many tools for attracting followers that everywhere he went people listened and left behind all that they knew and loved to follow him. With yarn or string, the family can create a net of care to attract "fish." Each strand can represent something that would attract people to God. Ask the family members to think of reasons that they practice their faith. Encourage them to discuss what people found and still find attractive about Jesus. As you build your net, feel free to add on to it. Hang it by the door or the ceiling of the entryway to remind you to always be "fishing."

January 28, 2018

Fourth Sunday in Ordinary Time

Hearing the Word

Mark 1:21–28

In the name of the Father, and of the Son, and of the Holy Spirit.

Then they came to Capernaum, and on the sabbath Jesus entered the synagogue and taught. The people were astonished at his teaching, for he taught them as one having authority and not as the scribes. In their synagogue was a man with an unclean spirit; he cried out, "What have you to do with us, Jesus of Nazareth? Have you come to destroy us? I know who you are—the Holy One of God!" Jesus rebuked him and said, "Quiet! Come out of him!" The unclean spirit convulsed him and with a loud cry came out of him. All were amazed and asked one another, "What is this? A new teaching with authority. He commands even the unclean spirits and they obey him." His fame spread everywhere throughout the whole region of Galilee.

Reflecting on the Word

The temptations and trials of daily life felt very much like real entities or "spirits" to contend with during the time of Jesus. When we see vice and sin as formidable entities to contend with, we take them much more seriously. They are not one-time choices, but forces that can hang over us like a cloud and confuse our judgment and decision making. We are not far from Lent. Perhaps now is the time to examine what forces have a hold on our thoughts and actions.

••••••ON THE WAY TO MASS:

What is something you want to bring into the presence of Christ in the Mass today?

ON THE WAY HOME FROM MASS: ••••••

Where and how did you experience the authority and presence of Christ in the Mass today?

Living the Word

All of us struggle with unclean spirits, but the authority of Jesus says they cannot stay with us if we don't want them to do so. They only stay with our permission. Invite family members to a water ceremony in which each person is invited to wash away something they are struggling with regularly. Each person can write something on a strip of paper with a washable marker, put the paper into a clear bowl with water and watch the colors run and dissolve into something beautiful. Explain that with God, all things can be made whole and beautiful again.

February 4, 2018

Fifth Sunday in Ordinary Time

Hearing the Word

Mark 1:29–39

In the name of the Father, and of the Son, and of the Holy Spirit.

On leaving the synagogue Jesus entered the house of Simon and Andrew with James and John. Simon's mother-in-law lay sick with a fever. They immediately told him about her. He approached, grasped her hand, and helped her up. Then the fever left her and she waited on them.

When it was evening, after sunset, they brought to him all who were ill or possessed by demons. The whole town was gathered at the door. He cured many who were sick with various diseases, and he drove out many demons, not permitting them to speak because they knew him.

Rising very early before dawn, he left and went off to a deserted place, where he prayed. Simon and those who were with him pursued him and on finding him said, "Everyone is looking for you." He told them, "Let us go on to the nearby villages that I may preach there also. For this purpose have I come." So he went into their synagogues, preaching and driving out demons throughout the whole of Galilee.

Reflecting on the Word

"For this purpose have I come," Jesus said. Jesus preached and healed. He did not build anything, or rule, or invent anything. Through his preaching and healing, other things were set into place. People who have been healed and have heard the Good News no longer live in fear or want. Communities who have heard the Gospel will come together to take care of each other's needs. We must have confidence in the good that flows from faith.

••••••ON THE WAY TO MASS:

Why did Jesus heal people?

ON THE WAY HOME FROM MASS: ••••••

Why did Jesus spend time in prayer before healing people?

Living the Word

Gather the family in the prayer space, light a candle, and ask for petitions for anyone who is unwell in any way. If it is appropriate, the family also can make cards or put a message in a get-well card to let the individuals know that you are praying for them. Discuss the power of prayer, and how Jesus still heals our bodies, minds, and souls. Tell the children that we take part in Jesus' healing ministry when we care for others.

Sixth Sunday in Ordinary Time

Hearing the Word
Mark 1:40–45

In the name of the Father, and of the Son, and of the Holy Spirit.

A leper came to Jesus and kneeling down begged him and said, "If you wish, you can make me clean." Moved with pity, he stretched out his hand, touched him, and said to him, "I do will it. Be made clean." The leprosy left him immediately, and he was made clean. Then, warning him sternly, he dismissed him at once.

Then he saide said to him, "See that you tell no one anything, but go, show yourself to the priest and offer for your cleansing what Moses prescribed; that will be proof for them."

The man went away and began to publicize the whole matter. He spread the report abroad so that it was impossible for Jesus to enter a town openly. He remained outside in deserted places, and people kept coming to him from everywhere.

Reflecting on the Word

The text presents a conundrum. Jesus clearly asks the leper to tell no one and yet he immediately tells everyone. It would seem if the leper were worthy of cleansing, then surely he would follow Jesus' command. Perhaps, healing is not contingent upon our dutiful following of every command. Jesus realizes that in our humanity we don't always live up to the gift of his love. Still, he gives his love freely knowing that at times we will follow and at times we will disobey.

•••••• ON THE WAY TO MASS:

If you were the leper, would you have told others about what Jesus did? Why or why not?

ON THE WAY HOME FROM MASS: ••••••

What does it mean to be clean on the inside versus the outside?

Living the Word

Propose to the family that a room be chosen to clean. Family members should see this cleaning as a chance to change the space both physically and with intention. For instance, if you clean the kitchen, rearrange things to promote hospitality or a feeling of nourishment. Or if you clear out a closet, use the time to think about clearing out space in your life and what needs to be cleansed that you have hidden away. You might decide that the family cleans a room together or that each family member may picks a room for cleaning. Either way, see how this can be turned into a cleaning of both the inside and outside.

February 18, 2018

First Sunday of Lent

Mark 1:12–15

In the name of the Father, and of the Son, and of the Holy Spirit.

The Spirit drove Jesus out into the desert, and he remained in the desert for forty days, tempted by Satan. He was among wild beasts, and the angels ministered to him.

After John had been arrested, Jesus came to Galilee proclaiming the gospel of God: "This is the time of fulfillment. The kingdom of God is at hand. Repent, and believe in the gospel."

Reflecting on the Word

"Believe in the gospel." In the middle of temptation and wild beasts, Jesus was still in the presence of angels. Perhaps this is where belief in the Gospel is at its fullest; right in the middle of both the good and the bad. Our belief calls us to truly change and grow, no matter what surrounds us. St. Paul reminds us that a faith without works is essentially dead. Lent is a special time to examine how we live out our faith among the good *and* the bad and to do something about it.

•••••• ON THE WAY TO MASS:

Have you ever experienced something good in the midst of a bad experience?

ON THE WAY HOME FROM MASS: ••••••

This is the start of Lent. What do you do differently during Lent?

Living the Word

Ask the family: How are we going to show our belief in the Gospel during this Lenten season? Are there things that we can do in our home to show that this is a time of renewal? While each person may have something specific in mind, see if there is anything you can do as a family as well. Perhaps, it is a simple prayer in the morning or giving up television, computers, and ipads, a few days a week to spend time volunteering or being together as a family.

February 25, 2018

SECOND SUNDAY OF LENT

Hearing the Word

Mark 9:2–3

In the name of the Father, and of the Son, and of the Holy Spirit.

Jesus took Peter, James, and John and led them up a high mountain apart by themselves. And he was transfigured before them, and his clothes became dazzling white, such as no fuller on earth could bleach them.

Reflecting on the Word

Who were you created in the image of and what are you here to do? Jesus and his disciples come face to face with this question as he was transfigured before their eyes. We finally see Jesus in all his splendid glory. However, he's not just called to be that dazzling figure on the mountaintop, he is also called to come down and be the Jesus who was crucified. This is often the way it is with us too; we are not called to be just one thing. It is never all glory or all suffering. Life is both.

• • • • • • ON THE WAY TO MASS:

We will hear today that Jesus' clothes were dazzling white. What does that mean?

ON THE WAY HOME FROM MASS: • • • • • •

If you had been there with Jesus on the mountain, would you have been like Peter and wanted to stay there? Or would you have been excited to come back down and do the work?

Living the Word

Encourage your family to try to see the fullness of those around them, instead of only as they usually think of them (as mother, sister, brother, etc.). As they look at family members more fully today, invite them to tell each other about the gifts that they notice that each possesses. At the end of the day, bring everyone together and ask if another's notice of a gift has changed how anyone feels about him or herself. Does this appreciation for a gift help anyone want to grow that gift and make it stronger? Would the family like to do this exercise again?

March 4, 2018

THIRD SUNDAY OF LENT

Hearing the Word

John 2:13–17

In the name of the Father, and of the Son, and of the Holy Spirit.

Since the Passover of the Jews was near, Jesus went up to Jerusalem. He found in the temple area those who sold oxen, sheep, and doves, as well as the money changers seated there. He made a whip out of cords and drove them all out of the temple area, with the sheep and oxen, and spilled the coins of the money changers and overturned their tables, and to those who sold doves he said, "Take these out of here, and stop making my Father's house a marketplace." His disciples recalled the words of Scripture, / *Zeal for your house will consume me.*

Reflecting on the Word

In today's Gospel, we notice that Jesus had strong emotions at times. The story illustrates how fully human Jesus truly was, and how if we are to be holy, we must fully embrace our humanness too. A full range of emotions is part of our humanity. It is what we do with our feelings that shows how connected we are to the divine. For instance, we should never act in anger, but rather feel the anger and use its energy to act out of compassion for self and others.

⋯⋯ ON THE WAY TO MASS:

Have you ever imagined Jesus as angry?

ON THE WAY HOME FROM MASS: ⋯⋯

What is something you feel passionate about changing? How would you go about doing that?

Living the Word

Acting in anger can be destructive so it's good to have ways to work through it. When we have such methods, actions motivated by your anger can come from a place of compassion. Talk with your family about what helps them feel calm and safe. Does taking a deep breath help them, or does it help to be in a quiet place? Can they use their anger to act in compassion? Could they stick up for someone being bullied or left out? As a family decide to take compassionate action on something this Lent.

March 11, 2018

Fourth Sunday of Lent

Hearing the Word

John 3:14–21

In the name of the Father, and of the Son, and of the Holy Spirit.

Jesus said to Nicodemus: "Just as Moses lifted up the serpent in the desert, so must the Son of Man be lifted up, so that everyone who believes in him may have eternal life."

For God so loved the world that he gave his only Son, so that everyone who believes in him might not perish but might have eternal life. For God did not send his Son into the world to condemn the world, but that the world might be saved through him. Whoever believes in him will not be condemned, but whoever does not believe has already been condemned, because he has not believed in the name of the only Son of God. And this is the verdict, that the light came into the world, but people preferred darkness to light, because their works were evil. For everyone who does wicked things hates the light and does not come toward the light, so that his works might not be exposed. But whoever lives the truth comes to the light, so that his works may be clearly seen as done in God.

Reflecting on the Word

Light figures prominently in this reading. We are told people avoid the light when they have something to hide. It's normal to want to hide our faults because we feel embarrassed or sad about them. However, we know things do not grow well in the dark and if we are to transform our faults and grow, we must bring all of ourselves into the warmth and energy of God's Light. There we find things look different and what we thought was too terrible to show anyone is actually transforming once bathed in the light of God.

・・・・・・ ON THE WAY TO MASS:

Do you sometimes like the darkness? Why?

ON THE WAY HOME FROM MASS: ・・・・・・

What does it mean to bring light to others?

Living the Word

Tonight light a candle for each family member, and as you do, speak of the ways you see God's love in them and how they are a light to others. Discuss how God's actions are always out of love and invite them to tell how they bring God's love to others. How might their actions light the way for another? Ask them to think of ways the family might share God's love and light as a unit. Is there a project in the church or neighborhood that all could do together?

March 18, 2018

Fifth Sunday of Lent

Hearing the Word

John 12:23–24

In the name of the Father, and of the Son, and of the Holy Spirit.

Jesus [said], "The hour has come for the Son of Man to be glorified. Amen, amen, I say to you, unless a grain of wheat falls to the ground and dies, it remains just a grain of wheat; but if it dies, it produces much fruit."

Reflecting on the Word

Jesus shows us how life and death are much more closely linked than one might think. We have been taught that they are opposites, but not so in this case. The life of a plant requires the death of a seed, the life of a butterfly requires the death of the caterpillar and so with us a new way of being in the world requires the death of bad habits, patterns of speech, and hurtful ways. Lent is a wonderful time to die to something that does not bear fruit in our lives.

•••••• ON THE WAY TO MASS:

What do seeds need to grow? How is light important to the growth process?

ON THE WAY HOME FROM MASS: ••••••

What "fruit" do you hope to have ready in time for Easter this year?

Living the Word

As we move into spring, plant some seeds as a family. This project can be as simple as planting a few grass seeds or herbs in a pot in your living room. As each member scatters their seeds, let them name something they wish to "die to" so that they may experience the joy of new life on Easter with Christ. Encourage everyone to notice the signs of spring all around as they go about their week and report back on them over dinner as they prepare to grow something new in their lives.

March 25, 2018

Palm Sunday of the Passion of the Lord

Hearing the Word

Mark 11:1-2, 7-10

In the name of the Father, and of the Son, and of the Holy Spirit.

When Jesus and his disciples drew near to Jerusalem, to Bethpage and Bethany at the Mount of Olives, he sent two of his disciples and said to them, "Go into the village opposite you, and immediately on entering it, you will find a colt tethered on which no one has ever sat. Untie it and bring it here. . . So they brought the colt to Jesus and put their cloaks over it. And he sat on it. Many of the people spread their cloaks on the road, and others spread leafy branches that they had cut from the fields. Those preceding him as well as those following kept crying out: / "Hosanna! / Blessed is he who comes in the name of the Lord! / Blessed is the kingdom of our father David that is to come! / Hosanna in the highest!"

Reflecting on the Word

This reading is in stark contrast to the Passion of Good Friday, but hints at what is to come with Easter. Putting today's "Hosanna!" next to "Crucify him!" is a difficult thing. How is it possible that Jesus was greeted gloriously and then tortured? The reality of Jesus' mission requires both. Our story, too, has joyful and painful times. We must be able to look to God during both times of joy and periods of struggle and sorrow. It requires much faith to hold the tension of both.

......ON THE WAY TO MASS:

Do you remember what will be special about today's liturgy?

ON THE WAY HOME FROM MASS: ......

How did you feel about participating at Mass in today? What is your favorite part of Holy Week?

Living the Word

Participate as a family in a Holy Week service. As a reminder of what this week is about and the tension of holding hope with fear, place the palms from today in a prominent place with some small slips of paper. Invite family members throughout the week to write something they hope for on one side of a slip of paper and something they fear on the other. On Saturday night, as the Easter fire is lighted, burn these papers to symbolize that you are giving them over to God.

April 1, 2018

Easter Sunday of the Resurrection of the Lord

Hearing the Word

John 20:1–9

In the name of the Father, and of the Son, and of the Holy Spirit.

On the first day of week, Mary of Magdala came to the tomb early in the morning, while it was still dark, and saw the stone removed from the tomb. So she ran and went to Simon Peter and to the other disciple whom Jesus loved, and told them, "They have taken the Lord from the tomb, and we don't know where they put him." So Peter and the other disciple went out and came to the tomb. They both ran, but the other disciple ran faster than Peter and arrived at the tomb first; he bent down and saw the burial cloths there, and the cloth that had covered his head, not with the burial cloths but rolled up in a separate place. Then the other disciple also went in, the one who had arrived at the tomb first, and he saw and believed. For they did not yet understand the Scripture that he had to rise from the dead.

Reflecting on the Word

As your *alleluias* ring out today, feel the spirit of rejoicing in every muscle and every cell of your body. For a moment, let go and feel what it is to be fully and completely basking in the glow of God's grace. So often we hold back from immersing ourselves in the liturgy. Wholeheartedly, allow the spirit of celebration to take over. As you sing and proclaim *alleluia* really mean it!

• • • • • • ON THE WAY TO MASS:

How do you like to celebrate?

ON THE WAY HOME FROM MASS: • • • • • •

What did you notice about how the church looked today?
How did it seem joyful?

Living the Word

As Mary ran to spread the Good News she didn't stop for a bite or to chat, but immediately went to the disciples who found it too good to be true and had to see for themselves. Ask family members if they have heard anything that sounds too good to be true and invite them to share it. Challenge each family member to spread this good news to at least five other people. Perhaps they will want to tell others!

April 8, 2018

SECOND SUNDAY OF EASTER / SUNDAY OF DIVINE MERCY

Hearing the Word

John 20:20b–23

In the name of the Father, and of the Son, and of the Holy Spirit.

The disciples rejoiced when they saw the Lord. Jesus said to them again, "Peace be with you. As the Father has sent me, so I send you." And when he had said this, he breathed on them and said to them, "Receive the Holy Spirit. Whose sins you forgive are forgiven them, and whose sins you retain are retained."

Reflecting on the Word

Through the breath of the Holy Spirit Jesus animates the souls of his disciples and sends them out to change the world. That same breath is always surrounding us everywhere we go. We simply need to intend to tap into it and we can also be filled with the Holy Spirit and the ability to preach and heal through our lives. This isn't a call reserved for the few. Imagine if with each breath we took, we blessed those around us. Such a blessing would transform how we see and are seen with each exhale.

······ ON THE WAY TO MASS:

How do you think the disciples felt when they saw Christ again?

ON THE WAY HOME FROM MASS: ······

What does it mean for the disciples to forgive or retain sins?

Living the Word

Gather the family in your prayer space and guide them through the following meditation: Take a deep breath in as you allow your eyelids to gently close. Notice how your eyelashes rest gently on your cheeks, the rise and fall of your breath, and the beating of your heart. For a moment, imagine yourself in a beautiful place in nature (the leader can elaborate here) and as you look to your right you notice a kind person beckoning you. As you approach, the person places his/her hands on your shoulders and gently breathes on the top of your head filling you with a warm white light. As you soak it in, notice every muscle, every cell feeling more relaxed and more alive.

April 15, 2018

THIRD SUNDAY OF EASTER

Hearing the Word

Luke 24:36–39

In the name of the Father, and of the Son, and of the Holy Spirit.

[Jesus] stood in [the disciples'] midst and said to them, "Peace be with you." But they were startled and terrified and thought that they were seeing a ghost. Then he said to them, "Why are you troubled? And why do questions arise in your hearts? Look at my hands and my feet, that it is I myself. Touch me and see, because a ghost does not have flesh and bones as you can see I have."

Reflecting on the Word

"Peace be with you" is such a powerful phrase. It does not promise that things will never go wrong or that we can completely control our surroundings. No matter what has or will happen, we can be at peace. If peace is simply with us, we can walk in the midst of the storm untroubled by the lightning strikes close to our feet. When we practice peace in all we do, we allow peace to make a home in our soul.

• • • • • • ON THE WAY TO MASS:

How do you live peace in your life?

ON THE WAY HOME FROM MASS: • • • • • •

Does anything threaten to steal your peace?

Living the Word

Practice peace today. Have the family choose an activity during which all will peacefully interact with each other in an almost exaggerated way. Everyone should feel free to have fun with this since humor is a close cousin to peace and often brings harmony to an intense situation. Perhaps you might compliment each other while playing a board game. Notice what it is like to live in peace. Was it easy, hard, enjoyable? Would family members like to try this during a dinner table discussion?

April 22, 2018

Fourth Sunday of Easter

Hearing the Word

John 10:14–16

In the name of the Father, and of the Son, and of the Holy Spirit.

[Jesus said:] "I am the good shepherd, and I know mine and mine know me, just as the Father knows me and I know the Father; and I will lay down my life for the sheep. I have other sheep that do not belong to this fold. These also I must lead, and they will hear my voice, and there will be one flock, one shepherd."

Reflecting on the Word

The Good Shepherd provides an example of leadership that shows compassion, care, and concern. There is an intimacy in the "knowing" that this shepherd has of his sheep. How different are the attributes show here than the image of other leaders? Do we see compassion as a strength or weakness in today's workplace, on the gym floor, or in the classroom? The goals of a shepherd focus on the sheep not the wool they will produce. Shepherds must tend and care for sheep daily without fail, for the wolves do not take a day off.

• • • • • • ON THE WAY TO MASS:

What is an example of a leader who is like a good shepherd?

ON THE WAY HOME FROM MASS: • • • • • •

How do you care for God's creation?

Living the Word

Today is Earth Day and one of our responsibilities as people of faith is to care for the earth and all of God's creation. Much like a shepherd tends his sheep so must we look after our precious resources. Invite the family to pledge to do something for the earth that shows they care. Track your progress on an earth chart throughout the week. See just how many things the family can do. Let this care be the family's prayer throughout the week.

April 29, 2018

Fifth Sunday of Easter

Hearing the Word

John 15:1–5

In the name of the Father, and of the Son, and of the Holy Spirit.

Jesus said to his disciples: "I am the true vine, and my Father is the vine grower. He takes away every branch in me that does not bear fruit, and every one that does he prunes so that it bears more fruit. You are already pruned because of the word that I spoke to you. Remain in me, as I remain in you. Just as a branch cannot bear fruit on its own unless it remains on the vine, so neither can you unless you remain in me. I am the vine, you are the branches. Whoever remains in me and I in him will bear much fruit, because without me you can do nothing."

Reflecting on the Word

Pruning is painful but necessary in our lives as well as in vineyards. However, when we remain connected to the vine, we do not have to do our pruning alone. Pruning is hard work, but it is possible and even can be comfortable in the context of community and through the grace of God's goodness. Daily we must make a choice to be connected to God. When we remain connected to our source, we can bear a seemingly infinite amount of fruit.

......ON THE WAY TO MASS:

Where do you feel most connected to God?

ON THE WAY HOME FROM MASS: ......

What does it mean to remain in God ?

Living the Word

Spring is a time of growth and new life. Take a walk as a family and observe the new growth all around you outside. You might ask the children if they notice that already some plants need to be pruned. As a family, work at home or volunteer to do yard work at the parish or for an elderly neighbor. See if there is a possibility of doing some planting. Spend some time in soil and appreciate the gifts of spring and the fruit all around you.

Sixth Sunday of Easter

Hearing the Word

John 15:9–10

In the name of the Father, and of the Son, and of the Holy Spirit.

Jesus said to his disciples: "As the Father loves me, so I also love you. Remain in my love. If you keep my commandments, you will remain in my love, just as I have kept my Father's commandments and remain in his love."

Reflecting on the Word

Remaining in love sounds like a wonderful thing. Why would anyone want to live any differently? So often people choose to see the bad things of this world instead of remaining steadfast in the infinite love of God. It seems like a difficult task with everything going on around us, but instead of calling us to a big change or something totally other, God simply asks us to stay. Stay in the love you were created out of, stay in the infinite vastness of the good within you. Simply remain.

......ON THE WAY TO MASS:

What anchors you to God's love?

ON THE WAY HOME FROM MASS: ......

Where have you experienced God's love today?

Living the Word

One of the main ways we experience love is through the power of appropriate touch. A hug from a friend, a hand on the shoulder for support, or snuggling on a cold day. As a family, create a circle of love and each take a turn being in the middle while everyone else has a hand on you. Feel the support of remaining in the love of God through your family. As you surround each person, pray a special prayer for the individual, either aloud or in your heart.

May 10, 2018

Solemnity of the Ascension of the Lord

Hearing the Word
Mark 16:15–16

In the name of the Father, and of the Son, and of the Holy Spirit.

Jesus said to his disciples: "Go into the whole world and proclaim the gospel to every creature. Whoever believes and is baptized will be saved; whoever does not believe will be condemned."

Reflecting on the Word

Jesus came not only for us humans but "to every creature." Therefore, as we take up the task of doing God's work in the world after the departure of Jesus we must remember to take that joyful news to all of God's creation in every way we can. Just as St. Francis would preach to the birds and considered even the sun and moon his brother and sister, so too must we make an effort to connect to all of the wonders God has done for us through the mission of our lives.

•••••• ON THE WAY TO MASS:

How can you proclaim the Gospel to parts of creation other than human beings?

ON THE WAY HOME FROM MASS: ••••••

Think about a story in the news that did not happen close by. How can you bring God's love to the situation from so far away?

Living the Word

We can preach in many far-reaching ways. Have the family walk through each room of your home, pausing to talk about how you can live out God's commission in every space of your life. Make sure to include all of creation in your reflection. For example, in the dining room someone may notice that cloth napkins can be used instead of paper towels to help save trees. Do you say prayers for others each night? If you have a backyard, do you have a birdfeeder?

May 13, 2018

Seventh Sunday of Easter

Hearing the Word

John 17:11b-12

In the name of the Father, and of the Son, and of the Holy Spirit.

Lifting up his eyes to heaven, Jesus prayed, saying: "Holy Father, keep them in your name that you have given me, so that they may be one just as we are one. When I was with them I protected them in your name that you gave me, and I guarded them, and none of them were lost except the son of destruction, in order that the Scripture might be fulfilled."

Reflecting on the Word

In God's love, there is no separation, so whatever happens to my sister or brother happens to me. The difference we feel now is simply an illusion that only holds sway on earth. We must strive to protect the most vulnerable among us, just as Jesus kept us safe. The true measure of a society is how well the vulnerable are taken care of. Let us be able to say "none of them were lost."

• • • • • • ON THE WAY TO MASS:

What would it be like to have zero separation from God?

ON THE WAY HOME FROM MASS: • • • • • •

Who is it hard to call sister or brother?

Living the Word

Search out songs from your family's experience and ones from other cultures and faiths that express that all are one. What do you notice about the universality of this message? What does it feel like to listen to the faith and culture of others and see it reflected in your beliefs? Ask your family to sit for a moment with that sense of connection and world-wide union. On at least one day this week, start the morning with one of the songs that you listened to.

Pentecost Sunday

Hearing the Word

John 16:12–14

In the name of the Father, and of the Son, and of the Holy Spirit.

[Jesus said to his disciples:] "I have much more to tell you, but you cannot bear it now. But when he comes, the Spirit of truth, he will guide you to all truth. He will not speak on his own, but he will speak what he hears, and will declare to you the things that are coming. He will glorify me, because he will take from it what is mine and declare it to you."

Reflecting on the Word

Truth has a power of its own, and when spoken, truth can act as guide and weapon. There is something about the truth, no matter how much people try to deny it, that can shatter any lie or illusion. The truth sets us free and at the same time binds us to right action. But, we must give the truth something to work with. If no one ever has the courage to proclaim it, its power will remain dormant and unused. Through the Spirit we can find the courage to be truth's voice in the world.

......ON THE WAY TO MASS:

What is something you know to be true?

ON THE WAY HOME FROM MASS: ......

What is the difference between a long-held belief and a stand-alone truth?

Living the Word

Most of us have swallowed a lie, and seen and felt the damage that it caused. This week have a truth liberation ceremony. Build a fire outside in a grill and have each person write down a lie that they no longer believe. As each person burns the old lie, have them proclaim aloud or to themselves the truth that has now replaced it. Take some time to discuss why we might believe a lie and how the context of community, especially one rooted in the love of God, can lead us back to the truth.

May 27, 2018

SOLEMNITY OF THE MOST HOLY TRINITY

Hearing the Word

Matthew 28:16–20

In the name of the Father, and of the Son, and of the Holy Spirit.

The eleven disciples went to Galilee, to the mountain to which Jesus had ordered them. When they saw him, they worshipped, but they doubted. Then Jesus approached and said to them, "All power in heaven and on earth has been given to me. Go, therefore, and make disciples of all nations, baptizing in the name of the Father, and of the Son, and of the Holy Spirit, teaching them to observe all that I have commanded you. And behold, I am with you always, until the end of the age."

Reflecting on the Word

Today we ponder the mystery and grace of the Most Holy Trinity. The great Franciscan scholar, St. Bonaventure, held this relationship at the forefront of his understanding of God. He maintained that God could only be understood in relationship, since by God's very nature, God is always in the relationship of the Trinity. Therefore, there is something about being made in the image of God that calls us to be connected to our fellow brothers and sisters in a deep and vulnerable way.

•••••• ON THE WAY TO MASS:

How do you experience God through your relationships with others?

ON THE WAY HOME FROM MASS: ••••••

How do you feel God will be with you, even "until the end of the age"?

Living the Word

Discipleship is practiced best with others. Jesus sent folks out two by two. Provide sheets of paper for family members. Ask them to write their names in the middle of the paper and then the names of important people in their lives. They should then draw an arrow pointing to those that they give something to and an arrow from those they receive something from. Encourage family members to notice the direction most of their arrows point and discuss ways that they feel others love and support them

June 3, 2018

Solemnity of the Most Holy Body and Blood of Christ

Hearing the Word

Mark 14:22–25

In the name of the Father, and of the Son, and of the Holy Spirit.

While they were eating, [Jesus] took bread, said the blessing, broke it, gave it to [the disciples], and said, "Take it; this is my body." Then he took a cup, gave thanks, and gave it to them, and they all drank from it. He said to them, "This is my blood of the covenant, which will be shed for many. Amen, I say to you, I shall not drink again the fruit of the vine until the day when I drink it new in the kingdom of God."

Reflecting on the Word

The Body of Christ can take many forms and we experience it in many ways. When we gather as the Church, we are the living Body. When we receive Communion, we participate in the Body, and when we live out our baptismal call, we are being the Body of Christ in the world. In each of the ways that the Body of Christ takes shape, we consider the presence of Christ. When we share Christ with others, we should be mindful of our *presence* in that moment of sharing.

• • • • • • ON THE WAY TO MASS:

Why is the Sacrament of the Eucharist so central to our faith?

ON THE WAY HOME FROM MASS: • • • • • •

For those who received Communion today what did you experience?

Living the Word

"We come to share our story, we come to break the bread" begins the Communion hymn "Song of the Body of Christ." Story and community are linked because in community we share our story and in community we act as the Body of Christ. Suggest that the family contact grandparents, other relatives, and close friends for a story-sharing circle. Relatives who are far away can be part of the circle by phone. Ask each person to share an important story from their life and end by together telling a story all of you know.

June 10, 2018

Tenth Sunday in Ordinary Time

Hearing the Word

Mark 3:31–35

In the name of the Father, and of the Son, and of the Holy Spirit.

His mother and his brothers arrived. Standing outside they sent word to him and called him. A crowd seated around him told him, "Your mother and your brothers and your sisters are outside asking for you." But he said to them in reply, "Who are my mother and my brothers?" And looking around at those seated in the circle he said, "Here are my mother and my brothers. For whoever does the will of God is my brother and sister and mother."

Reflecting on the Word

Over and over, Jesus' words and deeds call us to consider the oneness of our existence. Reserving the word "brother" or "sister" for only those related to us by blood or marriage fails to recognize the divinity in all that links us in ways we will never fully comprehend. Simply joining together in the will of God connects us in ways far more powerful than genetics. When we recognize this, we are able to build on it and make it stronger, using it for the benefit of all.

······ ON THE WAY TO MASS:

Who do you consider family?

ON THE WAY HOME FROM MASS: ······

What are five qualities that you feel are important for families to have?

Living the Word

Making a family tree can be a great way to reconnect to your roots. If a family tree already has been put together, spend some time exploring it. If it has not, many online resources can help. Each child can make a simple family tree for themselves. Find a way to include people who are not necessarily connected to you by blood but are a part of your family nonetheless. Talk about how we all have and need a family and what it means to be family to each other.

June 17, 2018

Eleventh Sunday in Ordinary Time

Hearing the Word

Mark 4:30–32

In the name of the Father, and of the Son, and of the Holy Spirit.

[Jesus said]: "To what shall we compare the kingdom of God, or what parable can we use for it? It is like a mustard seed that, when it is sown in the ground, is the smallest of all the seeds on the earth. But once it is sown, it springs up and becomes the largest of plants and puts forth large branches, so that the birds of the sky can dwell in its shade."

Reflecting on the Word

Nothing about Jesus' birth in the manger seemed to herald the king of heaven and earth. But from that humble beginning came a faith that changed everything. Power does not emanate from size or outward muscle but from a quality that is within the individual. If Jesus had allowed the stable to define him, he may have never had the courage to enter his full ministry. He knew that context is merely a backdrop for the full story yet to be written.

● ● ● ● ● ● ON THE WAY TO MASS:

What is something that looks small but can have a big impact?

ON THE WAY HOME FROM MASS: ● ● ● ● ● ●

What big things do you want to do?

Living the Word

Go on a small scavenger hunt as a family. This can be done around your house, the neighborhood, or somewhere in nature. See how many small things each person can find and, if appropriate, collect them. Once everyone has had a chance to seek out the small items, come together to share your findings and discuss how these small things affect our world in a large way. Ask the family: what are the small things about each other that go unnoticed but are vital to the family's well-being?

June 24, 2018

Solemnity of the Nativity of St. John the Baptist

Hearing the Word

Luke 1:57–66, 80

In the name of the Father, and of the Son, and of the Holy Spirit.

When the time arrived for Elizabeth to have her child she gave birth to a son. Her neighbors and relatives heard that the Lord had shown his great mercy toward her, and they rejoiced with her. When they came on the eighth day to circumcise the child, they were going to call him Zechariah after his father, but his mother said in reply, "No. He will be called John." But they answered her, "There is no one among your relatives who has this name." So they made signs, asking his father what he wished him to be called. He asked for a tablet and wrote, "John is his name," and all were amazed. Immediately his mouth was opened, his tongue freed, and he spoke blessing God. Then fear came upon all their neighbors, and all these matters were discussed throughout the hill country of Judea. All who heard these things took them to heart, saying, "What, then, will this child be?" For surely the hand of the Lord was with him.

The child grew and became strong in spirit, and he was in the desert until the day of his manifestation to Israel.

Reflecting on the Word

John clearly has an important role to play in the story of Jesus. From the beginning these men are linked. Elizabeth brought Mary tidings when John, even in the womb, recognized Jesus. However, his vital part can only be played if he chooses to do it. Therefore, we see that the acts and miracles of Jesus came from a network of courage and support through people like John and Mary and many others. We never know when our acts may be just as vital. The people in our life could have a profound impact on the world with our support, love, and guidance.

• • • • • • ON THE WAY TO MASS:

Is your name important to you?

ON THE WAY HOME FROM MASS: • • • • • •

How did you get your name?

Living the Word

There is power and much meaning in a name. In today's reading, we see how some wanted to call John a name that would not be his. Spend some time exploring the meaning of your full names. Explore both the meaning of the words and the family meaning in context. If anyone goes by a nickname, discuss that as well. Invite family members to make visual images of their names, reflecting their personality and likes, or a poem using each letter of their name to come up with a word.

Thirteenth Sunday in Ordinary Time

Hearing the Word

Mark 5:25–29

In the name of the Father, and of the Son, and of the Holy Spirit.

There was a woman afflicted with hemorrhages for twelve years. She had suffered greatly at the hands of many doctors and had spent all that she had. Yet she was not helped but only grew worse. She had heard about Jesus and came up behind him in the crowd and touched his cloak. She said, "If I but touch his clothes, I shall be cured." Immediately her flow of blood dried up. She felt in her body that she was healed of her affliction.

Reflecting on the Word

What an extraordinary story of courage and belief we hear in today's Gospel! Jesus tells the woman that her faith has saved her. Though this woman's hopes were dashed repeatedly and she had spent all her money on doctors that didn't help, she still found the courage to try again. Her faith was so strong she believed all she needed was to touch Jesus' clothes. Her determination never to give up and her ability to see Jesus as a healer serves as a model for our faith journey.

• • • • • • ON THE WAY TO MASS:

How would you describe your faith?

ON THE WAY HOME FROM MASS: • • • • • •

What in mind, body, or soul do I need to work on healing with divine help?

Living the Word

Ask your family if they have been inspired by anyone who has a chronic illness. Have they witnessed faith by the way the individual is able to maintain a joyful attitude despite the illness? How does this person portray hope to your family and others? As part of your prayer, ask God to continue to sustain the faith of these individuals. Allow time also for family members to consider how they treat adversity in their lives. Are they able to hand their problems over to God?

July 8, 2018

Fourteenth Sunday in Ordinary Time

Hearing the Word

Mark 6:4–6a

In the name of the Father, and of the Son, and of the Holy Spirit.

Jesus said to [his disciples], "A prophet is not without honor except in his native place and among his own kin and in his own house." So, he was not able to perform any mighty deed there, apart from curing a few sick people by laying his hands on them. He was amazed at their lack of faith.

Reflecting on the Word

In today's world what does it mean to be a prophet? We see in this passage that even Jesus had trouble being accepted among those he knew best. It is often much the same for us today. To be prophetic in our homes, churches, schools, and places of work, it takes great courage and resilience. Often our prophetic deeds will not be met with open hearts or much faith but that does not mean we should stop trying. Even small works of grace and mercy can have a big impact.

...... ON THE WAY TO MASS:

What is one message from God I could bring to friends or family this week by what I say or do?

ON THE WAY HOME FROM MASS: ......

Is there anywhere I lack faith and could be more open to good works? Whose good advice am I not listening to?

Living the Word

Make a list of good deeds (mighty or small) that as a family you would like to accomplish for people you already know this week. There is always need within our own walls and from the people we love. Does Grandma need the yard mowed? Is a brother or sister struggling with a project? What help does the mother or father need? Do these deeds without expecting appreciation.

July 15, 2018

Fifteenth Sunday in Ordinary Time

Hearing the Word

Mark 6:7–13

In the name of the Father, and of the Son, and of the Holy Spirit.

Jesus summoned the Twelve and began to send them out two by two and gave them authority over unclean spirits. He instructed them to take nothing for the journey but a walking stick—no food, no sack, no money in their belts. They were, however, to wear sandals but not a second tunic. He said to them, "Wherever you enter a house, stay there until you leave. Whatever place does not welcome you or listen to you, leave there and shake the dust off your feet in testimony against them" So they went off and preached repentance. The Twelve drove out many demons, and they anointed with oil many who were sick and cured them.

Reflecting on the Word

A similar passage in Matthew's Gospel (10:7–19) account inspired St. Francis of Assisi to give up his shoes and tunic and dress in the tunic and hood of the local shepherds. In such attire, he began preaching in the streets, a ministry that soon attracted many others. Francis and his brothers in the Friars Minor lived together and traveled throughout Italy preaching a message of repentance. It was important to Francis that they live among and of the people, owning nothing and begging for their every need.

• • • • • • ON THE WAY TO MASS:

Would you be able to be like the early Franciscans owning nothing and relying on God for everything?

ON THE WAY HOME FROM MASS: • • • • • •

How can we live out our call to go and serve those in need?

Living the Word

Take some time as a family to have a conversation with a vowed religious from an order. Is there a priest, brother, or sister in your community you could visit and ask about how they live the Gospel call to service? Perhaps they would be willing to share how they decided to commit themselves to that particular religious community. Ask them about what makes their community unique and if they are a local or an international community. You could also go online and read about the Franciscans or another order.

July 22, 2018

Sixteenth Sunday in Ordinary Time

Hearing the Word

Mark 6:30–34

In the name of the Father, and of the Son, and of the Holy Spirit.

The apostles gathered together with Jesus and reported all they had done and taught. He said to them, "Come away by yourselves to a deserted place and rest a while." People were coming and going in great numbers, and they had no opportunity even to eat. So they went off in the boat by themselves to a deserted place. People saw them leaving and many came to know about it. They hastened there on foot from all the towns and arrived at the place before them.

When he disembarked and saw the vast crowd, his heart was moved with pity for them, for they were like sheep without a shepherd; and he began to teach them many things.

Reflecting on the Word

When we look back over the lives of saints, we see, over and over again, how they took Jesus' message of rest and retreat to heart. St. Francis would often go away by himself to spend time in prayer and rejuvenation. He even had a small hermitage called the Carceri built in the hills above Assisi where he could go regularly. When we remove distractions and clutter, and spend time apart, we often are better able to hear God's voice in the simplicity and silence.

······ ON THE WAY TO MASS:

What do you hear when all is quiet?

ON THE WAY HOME FROM MASS: ······

Where do you go to find peace and quiet?

Living the Word

Take a retreat as a family. You may do this in your home or go somewhere special. During the retreat, family members should spend some time apart, some time in silence, and some time reading and/or journaling. Begin together with a prayer of intention and petitions, and end as a group with a song or recited prayer. Ask your family if they would like to open and close with a meal. Share the insights that came to you and notice how retreats are different from attending Mass and why saints found both to be an important part of their lives.

July 29, 2018

Seventeenth Sunday in Ordinary Time

Hearing the Word

John 6:11–15

In the name of the Father, and of the Son, and of the Holy Spirit.

Jesus took the loaves, gave thanks, and distributed them to those who were reclining, and also as much of the fish as they wanted. When they had had their fill, he said to his disciples, "Gather the fragments left over, so that nothing will be wasted." So they collected them, and filled twelve wicker baskets with fragments from the five barley loaves that had been more than they could eat. When people saw the sign that he had done, they said, "This is truly the Prophet, the one who is come into the world." Since Jesus knew that they were going to come and carry him off to make him king, he withdrew again to the mountain alone.

Reflecting on the Word

We so love miracles but we don't often realize our ability to help manifest them. Jesus did not bring the loaves and fish to begin with, he worked with what was already there and grew a miracle out of that. When we turn to God for help in desperate times, we must also start with what we bring to the table. What are we giving God to work with? If we give a little, in God's abundance we can end up with a lot.

•••••• ON THE WAY TO MASS:

Today we will hear about the multiplication of the loaves and the fish. Is there anything in your life that you would like multiplied?

ON THE WAY HOME FROM MASS: ••••••

What does it feel like to eat a big meal when you are very hungry?

Living the Word

Determine with the family a day this week for a meal of sharing. Instead of everyone preparing his or her plate and making sure they get enough, each family member prepares a plate for another. While food is put on plates, an abundance mentality should be kept in mind. As family members eat, they can share how they have experienced receiving more than enough in a situation where resources seemed limited at first. Notice if there are any leftovers and how many.

August 5, 2018

Eighteenth Sunday in Ordinary Time

Hearing the Word

John 6:32–35

In the name of the Father, and of the Son, and of the Holy Spirit.

Jesus said to [his disciples], "Amen, amen, I say to you, it was not Moses who gave the bread from heaven; my Father gives you the true bread from heaven. For the bread of God is that which comes down from heaven and gives life to the world." . . .

Jesus said to them, "I am the bread of life; whoever comes to me will never hunger, and whoever believes in me will never thirst."

Reflecting on the Word

We focus today on what sustains us. Jesus speaks of the "bread of life" and promises that, with this bread and our belief, we will never hunger or thirst again. However, we often choose to ingest unhealthy foods, media, and gossip and expect to live on them and then wonder why we are starving for true interactions, genuine affection, and kindness. We take in these things and then look no further, even though we are left hungry and slowly wasting away while eating dust.

•••••• ON THE WAY TO MASS:

How does Jesus feed us?

ON THE WAY HOME FROM MASS: ••••••

What could you eliminate from your "life diet" to feel healthier and full of life?

Living the Word

Take some time this week to bake a loaf of bread together as a family. Point out the role of the different ingredients and how yeast is used as a growing agent. Ask the children about the things that surround them and aid growth. Discuss how God's presence is always with us, surrounding us, and in us, providing us with a lifetime of material for growth. It is in and through God that we can truly be fed and feel full.

Nineteenth Sunday in Ordinary Time

Hearing the Word

John 6:44–51

In the name of the Father, and of the Son, and of the Holy Spirit.

[Jesus said:] "No one can come to me unless the Father who sent me draw him, and I will raise him on the last day. It is written in the prophets: *They shall all be taught by God.* Everyone who listens to my Father and learns from him comes to me. Not that anyone has seen the Father except the one who is from God; he has seen the Father. Amen, amen, I say to you, whoever believes has eternal life. I am the bread of life. Your ancestors ate manna in the desert, but they died; this is the bread that comes down from heaven so that one may eat it and not die. I am the living bread that came down from heaven; whoever eats this bread will live forever; and the bread that I will give is my flesh for the life of the world."

Reflecting on the Word

Eternal life is waiting for us but Jesus reminds us that we must believe to have it. We are active participants in our salvation. We see this as a great and wonderful gift but we must be prepared to believe. Belief is an individual choice that we are called to renew each day. Some days our faith might come easily and other days, it can seem harder to hold onto our beliefs. Again and again, we are called to trust in God through thought, word, and deed.

...... ON THE WAY TO MASS:

What does it mean to believe in something? What could make your belief in God stronger?

ON THE WAY HOME FROM MASS: ......

How does receiving God through the readings, Communion, and the community assembled feed you for the rest of the week? How can you participate more fully in the Mass?

Living the Word

Invite family members to decide each morning this week on a gift they will actively receive. A person could receive a gift by noticing the sunset, being more appreciative of friends, or thanking the cook for the meal. With this project, family members can do simple things to be more active in receiving. They can say thank you, eat slower, or leave earlier for a destination so they can take their time and be more appreciative of the journey. The experience of this active receiving can be shared around the dinner table.

August 15, 2018

Solemnity of the Assumption of the Blessed Virgin Mary

Hearing the Word

Luke 1:39–55

In the name of the Father, and of the Son, and of the Holy Spirit.

Mary set out and traveled to the hill country in haste to a town of Judah, where she entered the house of Zechariah and greeted Elizabeth. When Elizabeth heard Mary's greeting, the infant leaped in her womb, and Elizabeth, filled with the Holy Spirit, cried out . . . and said, "Blessed are you among women, and blessed is the fruit of your womb. And how does this happen to me, that the mother of my Lord should come to me? For at the moment the sound of your greeting reached my ears, the infant in my womb leaped for joy. Blessed are you who believed that what was spoken to you by the Lord would be fulfilled."

And Mary said: / "My soul proclaims the greatness of the Lord; / my spirit rejoices in God my Savior / for he has looked with favor on his lowly servant. / From this day all generations will call me blessed: / the Almighty has done great things for me / and holy is his Name. / He has mercy on those who fear him / in every generation. / He has shown the strength of his arm, / and has scattered the proud in their conceit. / He has cast down the mighty from their thrones, / and has lifted up the lowly. / He has filled the hungry with good things, / and the rich he has sent away empty. / He has come to the help of his servant Israel / for he has remembered his promise of mercy, / the promise he made to our fathers, / to Abraham and his children forever."

Reflecting on the Word

In this passage, we hear Mary's joy as she tells of the power and strength of God's love and goodness. Her words portray a God of action as she speaks of his justice and might. God's love is powerful for those whose belief is strong. Through faith and belief, we can become agents of change in the world. Mary's "yes" allowed God to bring change to the world through her.

••••••ON THE WAY TO MASS:

What have you said "yes" to lately? How did it turn out?

ON THE WAY HOME FROM MASS: ••••••

How could you apply something from the homily to your week?

Living the Word

Practice a form of *lectio divina* with the Gospel. In this exercise, the Gospel is read aloud three times. The second reading should be slower than the first, allowing for meditation on individual words, and the third reading should be even slower so that participants can pick out a word or phrase that stands out. Ask family members to depict their word or phrase through movement or posture, a drawing, or shared reflection. End by reading the passage a final time.

Twentieth Sunday in Ordinary Time

Hearing the Word

John 6:53-54

In the name of the Father, and of the Son, and of the Holy Spirit.

Jesus said to [the crowds], "Amen, amen, I say to you, unless you eat the flesh of the Son of Man and drink his blood, you do not have life within you. Whoever eats my flesh and drinks my blood has eternal life, and I will raise him on the last day."

Reflecting on the Word

To live eternally with Christ later, we need to take him in now as our nourishment. God sent Jesus to feed us. Do we accept him as the nourishment that brings eternal life? Are we willing to take in his Word and his Body and Blood in the Eucharist and allow him to change us? The life that we are offered through Christ prepares us for the banquet in heaven. Practicing our faith means allowing Christ to live in us so that we will become who we are, the Body of Christ.

•••••• ON THE WAY TO MASS:

How can you practice your faith even more fully than you do now?

ON THE WAY HOME FROM MASS: ••••••

What do you imagine it would be like to be fully in the presence of God's love and light?

Living the Word

Eternal is a concept that we don't often see lived out in our disposable culture. Take a trip to visit something in your area that has been around a long time. This could be a natural formation such as a cave, an ancient tree, or even an older adult in the neighborhood or a nursing home. Whatever you choose, take a moment to reflect on how the age of this thing or individual is only like a drop in the ocean compared to the eternity of heaven.

Twenty-First Sunday in Ordinary Time

Hearing the Word

John 6:68–69

In the name of the Father, and of the Son, and of the Holy Spirit.

Simon Peter answered [Jesus], "Master, to whom shall we go? You have the words of eternal life. We have come to believe and are convinced that you are the Holy One of God."

Reflecting on the Word

The disciples did not have the benefit of the Bible and the story of Jesus laid out for them. Can you imagine what it would be like to realize that your friend and teacher is indeed fully human but also fully divine? It must have taken courage for the followers to recognize their companion for who he truly was. Even when others could not see the truth, they stuck by his side and after his death continued to spread the Good News.

......ON THE WAY TO MASS:

What do you think Jesus would look like if you met him on the street?

ON THE WAY HOME FROM MASS: ......

Did you ever miss seeing something that was easily observed later? What was obstructing your view?

Living the Word

When we share insights of our experience of Christ, we help others see what they might not have. Ask each family member to draw a picture or cut out a picture from a magazine. Then ask each person to cut the picture into as many pieces as there are people in the family. If your family is small, you may want to cut more than one piece for each person. Next, pass out the pieces and invite each member of the family to identify the picture, based on the pieces in their hand. Put the pieces together and see who is right.

September 2, 2018

Twenty-Second Sunday in Ordinary Time

Hearing the Word

Mark 7:5–8

In the name of the Father, and of the Son, and of the Holy Spirit.

So the Pharisees and scribes questioned [Jesus], "Why do your disciples not follow the tradition of the elders but instead eat a meal with unclean hands?" He responded, "Well did Isaiah prophesy about you hypocrites, as it is written: / *This people honors me with their lips, / but their hearts are far from me; / in vain do they worship me, / teaching as doctrines human precepts.* / You disregard God's commandment but cling to human tradition."

Reflecting on the Word

We are reminded that God's ways are not human ways. Jesus catches people bending God to fit their understanding instead of seeking the fullness of God. Often we cling to what we know, but when we open ourselves to the truth of the divine, so much more is possible. A certain degree of freedom comes with the understanding that we do not have all the answers. When we can live in the mystery of the unknown, then we are truly able to hear God's commandment.

······ ON THE WAY TO MASS:

What is something you don't know about God?

ON THE WAY HOME FROM MASS: ······

Sometimes we hear Jesus' teaching differently and it seems new. Did anything in today's reading seem new to you today?

Living the Word

Ask your children about their expectations for the new school year. Is there anything that they would like to be different from last year? Encourage them to consider whether any of their expectations limit them. Give the children note cards and invite them to write down expectations, both good and bad, on one side of the cards. On the other side of the cards, they can write down what is possible with the help of God in each situation. How will including God keep their hearts close to him?

EVERYDAY FAMILY PRAYERS

The Sign of the Cross

The Sign of the Cross is the first prayer and the last: of each day, and of each Christian life. It is a prayer of the body as well as a prayer of words. When we are presented for Baptism, the community traces this sign on our bodies for the first time. Parents may trace it daily on their children. We learn to trace it daily on ourselves and on those whom we love. When we die, our loved ones will trace this holy sign on us for the last time.

In the name of the Father,

and of the Son,

and of the Holy Spirit. Amen.

The Lord's Prayer

The Lord's Prayer, or the Our Father, is a very important prayer for Christians because Jesus himself taught it to his disciples, who taught it to his Church. Today, we say this prayer as part of Mass, in the Rosary, and in personal prayer. There are seven petitions in the Lord's Prayer. The first three ask for God to be glorified and praised, and the next four ask for God to help take care of our physical and spiritual needs.

Our Father, who art in heaven,

hallowed be thy name;

thy kingdom come,

thy will be done

on earth as it is in heaven.

Give us this day our daily bread,

and forgive us our trespasses,

as we forgive those who trespass against us;

and lead us not into temptation, but deliver us from evil.

The Apostles' Creed

The Apostles' Creed is one of the earliest creeds we have; scholars believe it was written within the second century. The Apostles' Creed is shorter than the Nicene Creed, but it states what we believe about the Father, Son, and Holy Spirit. This prayer is sometimes used at Mass, especially at Masses with children, and is part of the Rosary.

I believe in God,

the Father almighty,

Creator of heaven and earth,

and in Jesus Christ, his only Son, our Lord,

who was conceived by the Holy Spirit,

born of the Virgin Mary,

suffered under Pontius Pilate,

was crucified, died and was buried;

he descended into hell;

and on the third day he rose again from the dead;

he ascended into heaven,

and is seated at the right hand of God the Father almighty;

from there he will come to judge the living and the dead.

I believe in the Holy Spirit,

the holy catholic Church,

the communion of saints,

the forgiveness of sins,

the resurrection of the body,

and life everlasting. Amen.

The Nicene Creed

The Nicene Creed was written at the Council of Nicaea in 325 AD, when bishops of the Church gathered together in order to articulate true belief in who Christ is and his relationship to God the Father. The Nicene Creed was the final document of that Council, written so that all the faithful may know the central teachings of Christianity. We say this prayer at Mass.

I believe in one God,

the Father almighty,

maker of heaven and earth,

of all things visible and invisible.

I believe in one Lord Jesus Christ,

the Only Begotten Son of God,

born of the Father before all ages.

God from God, Light from Light,

true God from true God,

begotten, not made, consubstantial with the Father;

through him all things were made.

For us men and for our salvation

he came down from heaven,

and by the Holy Spirit was incarnate of the Virgin Mary,

and became man.

For our sake he was crucified under Pontius Pilate,

he suffered death and was buried,

and rose again on the third day

in accordance with the Scriptures.

He ascended into heaven
and is seated at the right hand of the Father.
He will come again in glory
to judge the living and the dead
and his kingdom will have no end.

I believe in the Holy Spirit, the Lord, the giver of life,
who proceeds from the Father and the Son,
who with the Father and Son is adored and glorified,
who has spoken through the prophets.

I believe in one holy, catholic, and apostolic Church.
I confess one Baptism for the forgiveness of sins
and I look forward to the resurrection of the dead
and the life of the world to come. Amen.

Glory Be (Doxology)

This is a short prayer that Christians sometimes add to the end of psalms. It is prayed during the Rosary and usually follows the opening verse during the Liturgy of the Hours. It can be prayed at any time during the day.

Glory be to the Father

and to the Son

and to the Holy Spirit,

as it was in the beginning

is now, and ever shall be

world without end. Amen.

Hail Mary

The first two lines of this prayer are the words of the angel Gabriel to Mary, when he announces that she is with child (Luke 1:28). The second two lines are Elizabeth's greeting to Mary (Luke 1:42). The last four lines come to us from deep in history, from where and from whom we do not know. This prayer is part of the Rosary and is often used by Christians for personal prayer.

Hail, Mary, full of grace,

the Lord is with thee.

Blessed art thou among women

and blessed is the fruit of thy womb, Jesus.

Holy Mary, Mother of God,

pray for us sinners,

now and at the hour of our death.

Amen.

Grace before Meals

Families pray before meals in different ways. Some families make up a prayer in their own words, other families sing a prayer, and many families use this traditional formula. Teach your children to say this prayer while signing themselves with the cross.

Bless us, O Lord, and these thy gifts,

which we are about to receive from thy bounty,

through Christ our Lord.

Amen.

Grace after Meals

Teach your children to say this prayer after meals, while signing themselves with the cross. The part in brackets is optional.

We give thee thanks, for all thy benefits,

almighty God, who lives and reigns forever.

[And may the souls of the faithful departed,

through the mercy of God, rest in peace.]

Amen.